**Pictures
to share**

In the Garden
in pictures

for my sister Margaret;
the fairy at the bottom
of our garden.

**Pictures
to share**

First published in 2008 by
Pictures to Share Community Interest Company,
a UK based social enterprise that publishes
illustrated books for older people.

www.picturestoshare.co.uk

ISBN 978-0-9553940-5-8

In the Garden

in pictures

Edited by Helen J Bate

How do you like to go up in a swing

Up in the air so blue?

Oh I do think it's
the pleasantest thing

Ever a child can do!

Quotation from 'The Swing' from 'A Child's Garden of Verses'
by Robert Louis Stevenson (1850-1894)

The kiss of the sun for pardon,
The song of the birds for mirth,

**One is nearer
God's Heart
in a garden**

Than anywhere else on earth.

Painting: 'Garden by the Sea' by Mark Baring, contemporary artist
(Private Collection/The Bridgeman Art Library)
Small photograph: Butterfly © Vladimir Sazonov/istockphoto

Quotation from 'God's Garden' by Dorothy Frances Gurney (1858-1932)

Some flowers seem to smile;

some have a sad expression;

Photo: Garden flowers
© Geoff Dann/
Dorling Kindersley/
Getty Images

Quotation:
Henry Ward Beecher
(1813-1887)

The most beautiful things in the world

are the most useless;

peacocks and lilies for instance.

Quotation from 'The Stones of Venice'
by John Ruskin (1819-1900)

Happiness

isn't something you experience;
it's something you remember.

The most beautiful things in the world

are the most useless;

peacocks and lilies for instance.

Photograph: Peacock
©Marcelo Lerner/SambaPhoto/Getty Images

Quotation from 'The Stones of Venice'
by John Ruskin (1819-1900)

During a heatwave,

schoolboys from
Netherton Nursery School
in London cool off
in a spray of cold water.

Gardening requires lots of water,

most of it in the form of perspiration

Painting: 'A Corner of the Rose Garden at Bagatelle'
(oil on canvas) by Henri-Adolphe Laissement (1854-1921)
©The Bridgeman Art Library/Getty Images

Quotation: Lou Erickson. www.wisdomquotes.com

Blue tit

Wren

Bullfinch

Magpie

Thrush

Magpie

Goldfinch

Blackbird

One for sorrow
Two for joy

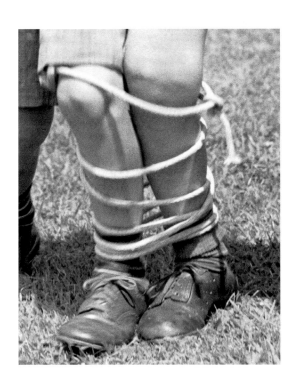

If you want to catch something,

running after it isn't always the best way.

The Bleaching Ground
by Max Liebermann (1847-1935)
Private collection/The Bridgeman Art Library

This is the weather the cuckoo likes;

And so do I;
When showers betumble the chestnut spikes,
And nestlings fly;

Main photograph: Common frog and common garden slug
©Tony Hamblin (rspb-images)
Small photograph: Hedgehog in grass. ©Rafal Olkis/istockphoto

Quotation from 'Weathers' by Thomas Hardy (1840-1928) from
A Puffin Book of Verse, Eleanor Graham, Penguin Books 1953

My love is like a red, red rose

That's newly sprung in June:
My love is like the melody
That's sweetly played in tune.

Painting: Detail from 'In Love' (oil on canvas) by Marcus Stone (1840-1921)
Nottingham City Museums and Galleries (Nottingham Castle)
The Bridgeman Art Library/Getty Images

Quotation: from 'A Red, Red Rose' by Robert Burns (1759-1796)
from the New Oxford Book of English Verse, Helen Gardner, Oxford University Press 1972

It's as large as life,

and twice as natural

Photographs: A pair of young girls dwarfed by a marrow grown on a Guildford allotment. Fox photo's/Hulton Archive/Getty Images

Quotation from 'Alice through the Looking Glass' by Lewis Carroll (1832-1898)

Don't count your chickens
before they hatch

Our England is a garden,

and such gardens are not made

By singing: 'Oh, how beautiful!'
and sitting in the shade,

While better men than we go out
and start their working lives

At grubbing weeds from gravel paths
with broken dinner knives.

Quotation from 'The Glory of the Garden' by Rudyard Kipling (1865-1935)

The North wind doth blow,

And we shall have snow,
And what will
the robin do then,
Poor thing?

He'll sit in a barn,
And keep himself warm,
And hide his head
under his wing,
Poor thing!

Photograph: Stuck Inside © Sharon Dominick/Istockphoto.com

Quotation: Traditional rhyme

January

brings the snow,

Makes our feet and fingers glow

Nothing is so beautiful as

Spring

Photograph: A sea of blue grape hyacinth and white daffodils.
© Darrell Gulin/Photographer's Choice/Getty Images

Quotation from 'Spring' by Gerard Manley Hopkins (1844-89)

A Canadian officer
stationed in Britain
planting sweetcorn
in the land surrounding
his military camp.

Spring
reflections

Painting: 'Spring reflections'
by Gerrit Greve,
contemporary artist
© Gerrit Greve/CORBIS

I go to

nature

to be soothed
and healed,

and to have
my senses
put in tune
once more.

Painting: 'Apple Blossoms - Spring' (oil on canvas) by Sir John Everett Millais (1829-1896)